Tax saving for the family business

Coopers
& Lybrand

Harrap London

1982 EDITION

First published in Great Britain 1982
by HARRAP LIMITED
19–23 Ludgate Hill, London EC4M 7PD
2nd edition: 1982

ISBN 0 245-53945-X

Designed by Robert Wheeler

Printed and bound in Great Britain
by Henry Ling Ltd, Dorchester

Contents

6 Looking to the future

Introduction

For the businessman to obtain the right taxation advice quickly, and therefore most cheaply, is always a matter of asking the right questions. In this book we set out the questions which, if they are not all the right questions for every family business, are at least those questions that are most often put to us.

There are six chapters in the book:

1 Starting a business
2 Tax planning for individual traders and partners
3 Tax planning for companies
4 Tax planning for directors and employees
5 Pensions for directors and employees
6 Looking to the future

These headings cover the main phases of the development of a business. We deal with the formation of a business, the problems that arise for continuing businesses and the individuals concerned with them, and the preservation of a business for future generations. Under each heading we ask the questions which seem to us to be important to most businesses.

We have answered these questions simply and have not aimed to write a detailed reference work. Our answers are not comprehensive and we must advise the reader against making any decisions without consulting his professional advisers. We hope, however, that this book will leave its readers with a greater understanding of how taxation affects the family business and better able to ask the right questions of their advisers.

The book which is now in its second edition takes account of legislation up to and including the Finance Act 1982.

1 Starting a business

Should I use a company from the outset?

The main reasons for trading through a company rather than as a sole trader or in partnership include:

- Limited liability. In practice this will not be fully achieved where company borrowing requires the support of personal guarantees from the directors. One way of avoiding the need for directors' guarantees is to use the government's scheme which provides loan guarantees for small businesses on loans up to £75,000. The scheme is operated by the banks, ICFC and certain other institutions.
- Continuity of ownership of the business. A company is in law a person separate from its owners and directors, so that legal ownership of the business is not affected by changes in ownership of the shares.
- Continuity of management. The management of a company may be separated from its ownership so that employees can reach senior positions without the shareholders disposing of the equity.
- Commercial relationships. Customers, suppliers and others, such as banks, normally prefer to deal with companies rather than individuals and partnerships. Companies are subject to statutory controls which give persons dealing with the company protection.

Companies are subject to the disciplines of the Companies Acts, which have no equivalent for the individual trader or partner. These include rules for keeping proper accounts and statutory records, for having an annual audit, forbidding loans to directors, and requiring that assets are used for the company's business.

The main disadvantage of using a company is that its shareholders do not own the company's assets. They have rights in the company and acting together can exercise full effective control over the company's affairs. Its assets, however, cannot be applied to the personal benefit of its shareholders or withdrawn from the business at will.

What are the initial tax considerations?

There are tax provisions designed to assist both individuals and companies at the start of a business:

- For individuals or partnerships, losses arising in the first four years of trading may be carried back and set against the individual's other income of the previous three years (see page 21).
- For companies, the 'business start-up scheme' described on page 15 allows an outside minority investor to deduct the amount of his or her investment (up to £20,000) in a qualifying company from taxable income.

A decision to use one or other of these reliefs may decide the question of whether or not a company should be formed.

Other tax considerations are against forming a company at the start of the business. These include:

- Trading losses of an individual or partner (including capital allowances and stock relief) may be offset for tax purposes against his or her other income (see page 21). By contrast, a company's trading losses may only be set against its own profits (see page 33).
- Cash can be introduced or withdrawn from the business without any additional tax implications. A company can transfer profit to its shareholders only by paying dividends which will be subject to tax in their hands as unearned income.
- National Insurance costs (and benefits) are lower for the self-employed than for employees (see page 25).

Are there any tax advantages in using a company?

The rates of tax at certain levels of profit are lower for a company than for an individual although even this advantage has been greatly reduced in recent years. The rates for 1982/1983 are compared as follows.

Income tax (individual)

Taxable income £	*Rate*
0—12,800	30%
12,801—15,100	40%
15,101—31,500	Between 45% and 55%
31,501 +	60%

Corporation tax (company)

Taxable profits £	*Effective rate*
0—90,000	40%
90,001—225,000	60%
225,001 +	52%

The marginal rate for companies compares favourably when profits are between about £19,000 and £90,000, or over £225,000.

The 40% rate of corporation tax is commonly known as the 'small companies rate'. It applies to profits below £90,000 but is withdrawn progressively as profits exceed this figure until at a profit level of £225,000 the standard rate of 52% applies. Between £90,000 and £225,000 the tax on any additional profit is at an effective rate of 60%.

A company enjoys certain other tax advantages, for example:

- The ability to offset trading losses against the chargeable capital gains of the year or the previous year. Individuals pay capital gains tax which is quite separate from income tax, and they cannot elect for a similar offset of trading losses.
- Payment of corporation tax is due nine months after the end of

an accounting period. Individuals pay tax on trading profits on 1 January of the year of assessment and 1 July following. This gives a company a comparative deferment of tax. On the other hand, the individual may benefit from paying tax on the profits of the prior year (see page 20).

• Trading losses of a company attributable to first-year allowances on plant and machinery may be set against profits of the previous three years. Losses for income tax may only be set against other income of the same or the following year (except in the first four years of trading).

• The rules for tax relief on pension contributions can be considerably more generous for employees, including directors, than for the self-employed; this is discussed further at pages 43 to 44.

The arguments for and against using a company on starting to trade seem finely balanced. What do you normally recommend?

This entirely depends on the taxation and financial circumstances of the proprietor. However, most businesses take time to become profitable and until this happens the tax rules favour the person trading as an individual or in partnership. It is always possible to transfer the business to a company at a later date but having done so it is much more difficult to transfer it back again (see pages 28 to 29).

Is there any advantage in using an unlimited company?

There are three advantages in using an unlimited company:

• No capital duty is payable on amounts subscribed for shares in an unlimited company.

• An unlimited company may purchase or redeem its share capital without restrictions imposed by the Companies Acts. The tax position however is the same as for a limited company (see page 35).

• An unlimited company does not have to file accounts with its annual return to the Registrar of Companies. A number of companies, including some very well known concerns, have been formed as or reregistered as unlimited companies for this reason.

The disadvantage of unlimited liability means that a shareholder on the Register at the time of liquidation and former shareholders who sold or transferred their shares within one year previously, may be called upon to meet any liabilities of the company not satisfied out of the proceeds of realisation of its assets. There is no question, however, of a member (or a former member) having to meet the company's liabilities whilst it remains a going concern.

Can I get tax relief for investing in my company's shares?

Generally speaking no. However, an individual who makes a loss on disposal of unquoted shares in trading companies for which he or she has subscribed may treat that loss as a trading loss, and set it off against other income of that or the following year. If the individual has other income this rule may cushion the risk.

You have mentioned the 'business start-up scheme'. What is this?

The business start-up scheme is intended to make it easier for new companies to raise equity capital from outside investors. New companies must meet certain requirements to qualify for the scheme. If all the conditions are met (and they are numerous) an outside investor who subscribes for ordinary shares in the company will obtain a deduction from his or her taxable income of up to £20,000 per annum. The main features of the scheme, which ends on 5 April 1984, are:

- The company must exist for the purpose of carrying on a bona fide new venture, and the shares must be issued within five years of its starting business.
- There is a minimum subscription of £500 per company (unless an approved investment fund is used as the vehicle) and a maximum allowance of £20,000 for 1982/1983 per individual investor, to which may be added any amount of the investor's allowance for 1981/1982 (£10,000) which he or she did not use in that year.
- Relief is limited to 50% of the ordinary share capital of each

company. If the relief is claimed by holders of more than 50% of the ordinary shares each claimant's relief is scaled down pro rata, subject to the rule that a claim which adversely affects an earlier claim will not be allowed without the consent of the earlier claimant.

• The company may not issue shares which are not fully paid up and its issued shares must be either:

(a) ordinary shares or ordinary non-voting shares (with otherwise identical rights); or
(b) fixed rate preference shares.

• The investor, together with his or her 'associates', may not hold more than 30% of the company. He or she may not have control, whether direct or indirect, nor have the right to obtain control. The term associate includes a spouse, partners and close relatives, but not a brother or a sister.

• The scheme is not open to employees (or persons who are partners of the company or their employees). The investor may be a director but may not receive payment for his or her services as such.

• Relief is not given until the company has carried on its trade for at least four months.

• Relief is denied if the scheme is used for tax avoidance. This general rule is reinforced by specific provisions which claw back relief retrospectively if value is received from the company or if the shares in the company are disposed of within five years.

• On a subsequent disposal of shares (outside the five year period), capital gains tax will be paid by the investor on any profit he or she makes. No relief for capital gains tax purposes will be obtained for any loss.

I can see that the rules are complicated. Can the scheme be made simple for my new company?

The complications have been introduced to prevent schemes of tax avoidance but, so long as the company's own arrangements are kept simple, it is not difficult to ensure that outside investors obtain the benefits that the Act intends.

What trades qualify?

A qualifying trade is a bona fide new venture which is not one of the businesses excluded by the Act. The Act excludes dealers in commodities, shares, securities, land or futures, and other dealers in goods who are not carrying on bona fide retail or wholesale businesses. It also excludes banking, insurance and financial activities, leasing activities, and the provision of legal or accounting services.

A trade is not a bona fide new venture if any person who controls it also controls another identical or similar business or if he or she controlled such a business more than five years previously. However, a business is not prevented from being a bona fide new venture if it is taken over from another person whether independent of the company and its controlling shareholders or not, but no business more than five years old can be regarded as new.

Am I right in saying that my relatives may not claim relief as investors in my company?

Yes, except that a brother or sister may qualify for relief.

How then do I find outside investors willing to subscribe for shares?

The legislation permits investment to be made by approved investment funds created to take advantage of these rules. Several such funds now exist and can provide equity funding (within the limits of the scheme) to qualifying companies. These funds can provide the individual investor with professional management and a spread of risks.

What is meant by the rule that relief is clawed back retrospectively if the investor receives value from the company?

The legislation is designed to prevent an investor obtaining relief and within five years afterwards receiving value from the company, for example, in the form of a redemption of his or her shares, a loan from the company, or repayment of a debt previously owed by the company, to name but a few of the transactions which are mentioned in the Act. Moreover, if the investor is a director, direct or indirect payment for services as a director will deny him or her relief.

No payment of whatever nature should be made to investors without taking professional advice.

2 Tax planning for individual traders and partners

How is an individual trader or partner in a partnership charged to tax?

The individual is liable to tax on all sources of income after deducting allowances and reliefs. Trading profits qualify as earned income (provided the individual personally acts in the conduct of the business), on which the highest rate of income tax is currently 60%.

A partner's liability to tax is calculated on his or her share of the partnership profits after taking into account individual allowances and reliefs, although the tax is then assessed and charged on the partnership and is a liability of the firm.

What are the rules for preparing accounts?

There is no legal requirement for an individual trader or partnership to prepare accounts although this information is certain to be required for commercial purposes. The Inland Revenue will require the preparation of a profit and loss account and balance sheet to support the income tax computation.

What are the main adjustments for tax purposes?

No item of capital expenditure can be deducted from profits, and expenditure which is not incurred 'wholly and exclusively' for the purposes of the business will be disallowed. This includes expenditure which is wholly or partly for private purposes.

Depreciation in respect of capital expenditure is also disallowed but a claim for capital allowances can be made for any expenditure on assets which qualify. Details of these are given on page 22.

Certain items, such as entertaining (except entertaining of foreign customers or staff), are disallowed by law whether or not incurred for business purposes. Amounts set aside for expenditure not yet incurred, such as a provision for future repairs, will be disallowed although such items may be claimed as and when they are spent.

Relief is given for inflationary increases in the value of trading stock over the period of account (see page 23).

What is the basis of assessment?

Income tax is assessed for the year ended 5 April (the 'fiscal year'). The taxable profits of a person carrying on a trade either alone or in partnership are assessed to income tax on a preceding year basis (the 'prior year' basis). This means that the accounts of a financial year ending in the previous tax year will determine the assessment of the following fiscal year.

When a business starts, this prior year basis is impossible and the actual profits for the fiscal year are assessed. There are rules for moving from an 'actual' basis to the prior year basis in the first three years or so of trading, which can result in certain profits being assessed more than once and other profits escaping assessment. The taxpayer has an option in deciding the year in which to move onto the prior year basis. These rules can mean that the aggregate of the profits assessed to tax in the early years is less than the profits earned and advice must be taken to ensure that the best tax result is achieved.

When a business ceases the actual profits in the year of cessation are assessed. The Inland Revenue also has an option of assessing the previous two fiscal years on an actual basis (rather than the prior year basis).

To obtain the maximum deferment from the time profits are earned until they are assessed to tax, an advantage may lie (depending on the trend of profits) in having an accounting date early in the fiscal year starting 6 April. The profits will then be assessed to tax on the prior year basis for the following year. This can be seen from the following example.

Period of accounts	*Fiscal year in which the accounts end (the 'prior year')*	*Fiscal year for which accounts are assessed*
Year to 30 June 1981	1981/1982	1982/1983
Year to 31 March 1981	1980/1981	1981/1982

The prior year basis has been criticised both for its complexity and its possibilities for legal tax avoidance, and has been under review by the Inland Revenue for some time. Meanwhile, for any business where profits are growing (whether as a result of inflation or in 'real' terms), the prior year basis is likely to be beneficial over a number of years because its effect is that the assessment for any one year is based on the (generally lower) profits for the previous year.

What happens if I make a loss?

Even a profitable trade may show an adjusted tax loss, as a result of capital allowances and/or stock relief. A tax loss may be set against any other income of the taxpayer for the tax year in which the loss is made and, if unrelieved in that year, may be set against other income of the following tax year. Any loss still not relieved can only be set against future profits of the same trade.

During the first four tax years in which the trade is carried on, a claim can be made to set losses against any of the taxpayer's income in the three tax years before the loss arose, taking the earliest year first. This rule can cover some of the financial risk in starting a new trading venture.

In claiming these reliefs, the taxpayer must show that he or she was carrying on the trade on a commercial basis with a view to profit. This will exclude certain hobby businesses but most traders will meet the test. There are special rules which restrict the relief for losses from farming where a loss has been incurred in each of the previous five years.

What tax relief is given on expenditure incurred before the business starts?

There are separate rules for capital and revenue expenditure:

• For capital allowance purposes money already spent on capital assets is deemed to be incurred at the start of trading, and the normal allowances are given in the opening period.

• Allowable revenue expenditure incurred up to three years before trading starts (but not before 1 April 1980) is treated as a loss sustained in the opening year of assessment.

What are the allowances given for capital expenditure?

Allowances against profits for capital expenditure ('capital allowances') are given at the rates set out in the table below (expenditure from 11 March 1981).

Main classes of capital allowances

	Initial allowances %	*First-year allowances* %	*Writing-down allowances* %
New and second-hand plant and machinery	—	100 (a)	— (c)
New and second-hand private cars	—	— (b)	25 (c) (maximum £2,000 pa)
Other new and second-hand vehicles	—	100 (a)	— (c)
Scientific research (including buildings)	—	100	—
Industrial buildings purchased new in the period - up to 2,500 sq ft (e)	100 (a)	—	— (d)
- other	75 (a)	—	4 (d)
Agricultural buildings and works	20 (a)	—	10 (d)
Qualifying hotels	20	—	4 (d)
Patent rights	Written off over 17 years (straight line) or remaining life of patent if less		
Second-hand industrial buildings	Special rules apply		
Dwellings let on assured tenancies (from 9 May 1982) by approved bodies	Special rules apply		
Ships	Special rules apply		
Mines, oil wells etc	Special rules apply		
Know-how	Special rules apply		

Notes

(a) These initial and first-year allowances may be disclaimed wholly or in part, in which case writing-down allowances at 25%, except where otherwise shown, will be available.
(b) First-year allowances can be claimed on cars in a limited number of cases.
(c) Writing-down allowances are given on the reducing balance basis.
(d) Writing-down allowances are given on the straight line basis.
(e) 1,250 sq ft for expenditure incurred after 26 March 1983.

Enterprise zones
The capital allowances shown in the table above may be accelerated if expenditure is incurred on industrial, commercial or hotel buildings in areas designated 'enterprise zones'.

Businesses operating in such zones qualify for other benefits including exemption from development land tax, general rates and training levies.

The 100% allowances on machinery or plant or on scientific research are given for expenditure on new or second-hand assets, unless the buyer and seller are connected. The allowances on buildings are given when expenditure is incurred on construction and there are special rules when a building is purchased second-hand.

What is stock relief and how is it given?

Stock relief is a deduction from trading profit which is intended to reflect increases in stock values in the period of account due to inflation.

Under the current rules, which apply to accounting periods ending on or after 14 November 1980, the deduction is calculated by applying the percentage movement in an index (known as the 'all stocks index') to stock values at the beginning of the period of account.

Stocks are defined as 'property such as is sold in the ordinary course of the trade' (including work in progress) and materials used in the manufacture, preparation or construction of such property. Securities, land and buildings (other than land or buildings held for development), and leased assets do not qualify. The first £2,000 of stock is excluded.

The following is an example of the calculation of stock relief.

Accounts—year to 31 December 1981	
Stock value—31 December 1980	£102,000
Stock value—31 December 1981	£65,000
Movement on the all stocks index in year to 31 December 1981 is 9.17%.	
Stock relief for year to 31 December 1981	
Opening stock	£102,000
Less	(2,000)
	£100,000
Relief (9.17% of £100,000)	£9,170

There is now no clawback of relief when stocks fall (as there was under the original stock relief rules) but if the business ceases relief granted for the previous six years will become chargeable to tax. Relief is similarly recovered if the activities of a trade become negligible in comparison with the scale at any time in the previous six years. This rule is intended to catch cases where the business is kept going at a minimal level to avoid the clawback of relief.

Will it save tax if I introduce members of the family as partners?

Where members of the family are able to make a contribution to the business there will be savings achieved by distributing profits among a number of individuals who will each benefit from the lower bands of tax. A wife may elect for separate taxation of earned income. The member of the family thus introduced will accept the risks of the business and must personally act in the conduct of the business (as opposed to taking a purely financial interest) if his or her income is to be treated as earned.

The introduction of a new partner into a business (whether a member of the family or some other person) means that the business is deemed to cease for tax purposes and to recommence, unless all persons engaged as partners in the business both before and after the change elect that the business should be treated as continuing. The effect of a cessation and recommencement is briefly described on page 20. There are certain circumstances where a cessation can be beneficial, and other circumstances where a cessation gives rise to substantial additional tax. In all circumstances professional advice must be taken.

What is my responsibility for tax on employee salaries?

All employees are subject to tax under Schedule E on their income from employment. The law imposes upon the employer responsibility under the Pay As You Earn (PAYE) system for deducting Schedule E income tax from all payments of wages, salaries or other remuneration, and paying the tax over to the Inland Revenue. This applies even if there is only one employee, for example a wife paid a salary by her sole trader husband. The PAYE branch of the Inland Revenue issues full instructions to employers for calculating PAYE deductions weekly or monthly and for reporting expenses and benefits paid to employees (see page 42).

Will National Insurance contributions be payable also?

National Insurance contributions are really a form of additional income tax, although the social security and income tax systems have always been kept separate. Payment of contributions as part of the PAYE system is compulsory under the Social Security Acts.

Contributions are payable under four classes according to the status of the individual:

- Class 1. For employees. Contributions are payable both by employees and employers as part of the PAYE system.
- Class 2. Paid by the self-employed.
- Class 3. Voluntary contribution (made for example by persons overseas) to maintain qualification to certain benefits, mainly the retirement pension.
- Class 4. Paid by the self-employed.

The total cost of Class 1 contributions for employees is usually much greater than the combined cost of Class 2 and Class 4 contributions for the self-employed. Employees may in return claim certain benefits not available to the self-employed (unemployment benefit, earnings-related sickness and pension supplement, industrial injuries benefit).

How does the self-employed person make arrangements for a retirement pension?

A self-employed person will qualify for the basic State pension only and not the earnings-related pension. For anything further the self-employed must make their own arrangements.

The self-employed person is entitled to tax relief for contributions ('Retirement Annuity Premiums') he or she makes under a retirement annuity contract up to a limit of 17½% (increased to 20% for persons over 50 with higher percentages for persons over 68) of his or her earnings (as defined). The income received by the pension fund will then build up tax free.

The pension benefits derived from the scheme may include:

- Life assurance cover.
- Pension payable from any age between 60 and 75.
- Pension for spouse or dependants on death.
- Tax free lump sum up to three times annual pension, payable when the pension starts.

Saving for retirement in this way is very tax efficient and any self-employed person should consider paying the maximum contribution that he or she can afford within the permitted limits.

When is VAT registration necessary?

Registration is compulsory for individuals, partnerships and companies supplying goods or services in the United Kingdom in the course of a business where the expected value of turnover in a year will exceed £17,000 or where the turnover has exceeded £6,000 in a quarter. These limits mean that most businesses are required to register and where the need to register is foreseen it will be necessary to make prompt application.

It will usually be to the advantage of a business with a turnover of less than £17,000 to elect to register voluntarily if its sales are mainly to other registered businesses. By registering it can recover VAT paid on its inputs (that is cost of goods and services) whilst its customers will be able to recover the VAT charged on its sales. Since VAT is borne by the ultimate consumer small traders selling to the general public will usually benefit if they do not have to register and charge VAT.

There are certain categories of supplies on which VAT is not chargeable and these are known as 'zero-rated' or 'exempt' supplies. The main difference between a zero-rated and an exempt supply is that a business making zero-rated supplies can recover VAT paid on inputs whilst a business making wholly exempt supplies cannot. Examples of zero-rated supplies are supplies of food and exports. You should obtain professional advice on whether the rules applying to these supplies are relevant to your business.

There are special schemes to assist retailers to account for VAT on goods which fall into different categories. It is worth obtaining from Customs and Excise their two main booklets: 'VAT: General Guide (Notice No: 700)' 'VAT: Scope and Coverage (Notice No: 701)'.

How does capital gains tax apply to business assets?

The sole trader will be liable to capital gains tax on any gain arising from the sale of a chargeable business asset (for example land, buildings or goodwill). A partner will be similarly liable on the proportionate part of the gain attributable to him or her from the sale of partnership assets, which may include gains arising on withdrawal from a partnership where he or she disposes of a share of the assets to the other partners.

The Finance Act 1982 has introduced a degree of indexation of costs of assets subject to capital gains tax on disposal. This is described more fully on page 50.

The charge to tax on business assets can be deferred by claiming what is generally called 'rollover relief'. This relief can be claimed in respect of gains arising on the sale of assets provided that the proceeds of sale are reinvested in 'new assets' acquired for use in the trade, and both old and new assets fall within the following classes:

- Buildings or land occupied (as well as used) only for the purposes of the trade.

- Fixed plant or machinery.
- Ships, aircraft and hovercraft.
- Goodwill.

Expenditure on the new assets must normally be made within the period of four years starting 12 months before the disposal of the old assets. This period may be extended at the discretion of the Inland Revenue.

Is development land tax likely to be important?

Development land tax (DLT) is charged on the 'realised development value' of land (including buildings) in the United Kingdom. This refers to the increase in value of land or buildings attributable to a change of use requiring planning permission. The occasions of charge are:

- Sales of any interests in land or buildings (which are deemed to include the grant of a lease).
- Start of development.
- Certain changes of use.

There are rules which require the notification of the start of a material development, whether or not tax will arise.

The first £50,000 of chargeable development gain for each year (to 31 March) is exempt from tax and the balance is chargeable at the flat rate of 60%. The exemption of £50,000 which is given separately to both husband and wife will leave many smaller businesses unaffected by DLT.

Can I transfer my business as a going concern into a company?

This will normally be possible at little additional tax cost provided that the entire trade is transferred in exchange for shares in the company. There are, however, three unavoidable results of such a transfer:

- When an individual or partnership ceases to trade, the prior year basis of assessment to tax is set aside and profits in the final year of assessment will be taxed on an actual basis (see page 20). In addition the Inland Revenue has the right to assess the two previous years on the actual instead of the prior year profits. Where profits are steadily rising this will create a liability to tax which would otherwise be avoided or deferred.

- Stamp transfer duty at 2% of market value will be payable on assets transferred to the company, other than those which can pass by physical delivery (there are lower rates where the total value of assets is not greater than £40,000). The charge will normally exclude stocks and most machinery, but will cover land, buildings and fixtures, goodwill, debtors and investments.
- Capital duty will be payable at 1% on the value of the net assets contributed to the company in exchange for the company's shares.

Capital and stamp duties may in practice be the heaviest cost of incorporation.

Can a company pass its business back to the individual shareholders as a going concern?

In most cases this would be an expensive exercise under existing tax legislation, although it may be possible if the company has been incurring losses, or the scale of its business is small.

Shareholders can expect to benefit from their investment in the company either by receiving dividends or by realising a capital profit from a sale of their shares or the ultimate dissolution of the company. The transfer of a business as a going concern by a company to its shareholders will probably be frustrated by the tax rules:

- Any values of the assets in excess of the original value subscribed for the shares may be treated as a dividend.
- If the company is liquidated the shareholders will be treated as disposing of their shares for capital gains tax purposes.
- The transfer of assets will be a chargeable capital disposal by the company.

One way or another the extraction of funds from a company will give rise to tax liabilities, which in the case of a successful business are likely to be considerable. It is unlikely that the new reliefs for a company purchasing its own shares (see page 34) will be of much assistance.

3 Tax planning for companies

Is corporation tax separate from income tax and capital gains tax?

Yes. Companies pay corporation tax on both income and capital gains. The capital gains are reduced by a fraction and then added to the profits chargeable to corporation tax. The effective rate of corporation tax on chargeable gains is 30%, which is the same as the capital gains tax rate.

Corporation tax therefore replaces both income tax and capital gains tax as a charge on the profits of companies. If the company pays dividends out of profits which have suffered corporation tax, additional income tax may be paid by shareholders.

How is corporation tax charged and paid?

The rates of corporation tax are set for each 'financial year' which ends on 31 March. The tax is assessed on a company for its accounting periods which are normally the periods for which it prepares accounts. Where the accounting periods fall into different financial years the profits are apportioned and charged at the appropriate rates.

Corporation tax is paid by most companies nine months after the end of the accounting period. Certain companies which have continued to trade since 1964 or earlier have longer periods for payment.

How are dividends treated?

When a company pays a dividend it must pay an amount of advance corporation tax (ACT) at a rate which is related to the basic rate of income tax. For 1982/1983 the basic rate is 30% and the ACT rate is three-sevenths, so that if a dividend of £70 is paid the ACT will be £30. The ACT is called a 'tax credit' and is added on to the net dividend to determine the shareholder's gross income. In the above example the shareholder is treated as having gross income of £100 on which tax of £30 has been accounted for.

The company will treat the ACT as a payment on account of its liability to corporation tax, so that although the payment of tax is brought forward no additional tax is payable. However, for a company which is not otherwise paying corporation tax (for example, because of unused capital allowances) payment of ACT is an additional cost of paying dividends.

Will not dividends be expensive in tax for the shareholders?

No additional tax is payable by the shareholder if his or her income (including the dividend) is taxed only at the basic rate. The dividend, however, is unearned income on which investment income surcharge (at 15%) will be paid where the individual's net investment income exceeds the threshold, currently £6,250.

Above this threshold the tax cost of paying dividends climbs steeply so that there is every tax incentive to retain profits in the company.

Waivers of dividends by certain shareholders may be feasible if a distribution of income disproportionate to the shareholdings in the company is desired. This is a matter on which professional advice should always be obtained.

What level of salary should the company pay to the shareholder directors?

The decision should not really be made for tax planning reasons, although tax is often a major factor:

- The company will get a deduction for tax purposes for salaries which are paid wholly and exclusively for the purposes of the trade, and not merely to suit the tax arrangements of the shareholders. Salary levels must, therefore, be justifiable in relation to services performed. This is, however, a subjective matter where judgement may be exercised within fairly wide limits.

- Shareholder directors in an expanding company will often take less than commercial salaries to help the company's finances. Salary levels in future years cannot be justified by reference to salary forgone in the past, and if payment of salary is tax effective it is possible to lend the cash back to the company.
- Payment of salary to shareholder directors will be tax effective if relief to the company for corporation tax is at least equal to the additional tax payable by the individual. At certain profit levels the company's marginal rate and the individual's top rate on earned income are the same (that is 60%—see page 13). If the company's rate is the standard rate there will be only an 8% difference between the top rate of tax on the salary (at 60%) and the relief to the company (at 52%). Increasing salary levels is likely to represent a cheaper way of extracting funds than payment of dividends.

What is a 'close company'?

A close company is one which is 'controlled' by five or fewer 'participators' (shareholders, with holdings aggregated with those of their associates) or by any number of directors. In practice nearly all family companies are close companies.

How important is close company legislation nowadays?

The purpose of close company legislation in the past has been to prevent the avoidance of the higher rates of income tax by retaining profits within a company taxed at the lower corporation tax rates, instead of distributing them to the shareholders. This purpose was achieved by rules which apportioned profit to shareholders whether it was distributed or not.

The Finance Act 1980 abolished the apportionment of the trading income of close companies so that close company legislation for the most part has ceased to be severe. Companies still have to distribute their investment income and half their estate income (for example, rental income received by property investment companies) unless, in the case of trading companies, they can show a business need to retain it. Their shareholders will suffer apportionment of this income unless the distribution is adequate.

The relaxation of apportionment of trading income means that there are no real disadvantages for a trading company or a trading group in being close. Moreover there is one significant advantage in that tax relief is given to an individual on interest on a loan used to acquire shares in or lend money to a close company, provided that he or she either has a material interest in the company (more than 5% of the equity) or holds some part of the ordinary share capital (which may be less than 5%) and is a full time working director or employee. This rule can be critical where individuals are buying shares or considering additional investment in a close company. The company must be close when the investment is made; it matters not if it subsequently becomes 'open'.

If a close company makes loans to participators it must pay tax at three-sevenths of the loan, the current rate of ACT (see also page 39). This tax payment is recoverable when the loan is repaid.

What happens if the company has losses for tax purposes?

The company can use its trading losses to cover all other profits (including chargeable capital gains) of the period, or of the previous period. A loss attributable to first-year allowances on plant can be set against profits of the three years prior to the year of loss provided that the company has been carrying on the same trade for those years. Unused losses will be carried forward and can only be used to cover future trading income from the same trade.

Capital losses can only be offset against chargeable capital gains.

Is there any way the shareholders can benefit from the company's losses?

There is no direct way of the shareholders obtaining any benefit in the form of relief for the company's loss.

Are there any indirect means of the shareholders benefiting: by the sale of the company for instance?

There are special rules by which losses carried forward may be disallowed where there is a change of ownership of a company. This means that an intending purchaser of a company will be wary of regarding unrelieved tax losses as an 'asset' (although with careful planning they may often be preserved) so that the vendors always have difficulty in obtaining any additional consideration for the loss.

A shareholder who has subscribed for shares in an unquoted trading company may obtain some tax benefit if he or she makes a loss on disposal of those shares (see page 15). The shareholders can relieve the company of financing charges by borrowing money themselves and either lending to the company interest free or investing the money in the company's shares. Either way a shareholder holding more than 5% or working full time for the company should obtain relief for the interest (see page 32).

Can a company purchase its own shares?

The Companies Act 1981 permits limited companies, if empowered by their articles, to purchase their own shares subject to certain safeguards. The company must purchase the shares out of profits available for payment of dividends or out of a new issue of shares made for the purpose.

A private company (but not a public company) may then buy in its shares out of capital (once it has used its distributable profits) but subject to stringent safeguards for the protection of shareholders and creditors. These safeguards include:

- Statutory declarations of solvency to be made by the directors (and reported on by the auditors) which must also cover the company's ability to remain a going concern for the following year.
- Publication in the gazette and the national press.
- Rights of creditors or dissentient shareholders to object.
- Provisions whereby past members and the directors may have to contribute to the assets to the extent of the payment out of capital if the company becomes insolvent.

Unlimited companies may buy or redeem their own shares without restriction.

What are the taxation effects?

The general tax rule is that any payment made by the company to its shareholders in the purchase of its own shares will be treated as a distribution (which means that it will be taxed as if it is a dividend), except to the extent that the shareholder is receiving back the amount subscribed for the shares. The Finance Act 1982 provides that, in certain circumstances, an unquoted trading company may purchase its own shares without its shareholders being treated as if they had received a dividend. The shareholder, however, must bring the proceeds into his or her capital gains tax computation. The new relief will apply to:

- Payments to shareholders applied towards payment of capital transfer tax liabilities arising on death (but only in cases of hardship).
- Purchases or redemptions of shares made wholly or mainly to benefit the trade and not designed for the purposes of avoiding tax.

There are certain conditions that the shareholder must meet which are that he must be resident in the United Kingdom and have owned his shares for at least five years, and his percentage holding in the company must be substantially reduced by at least 25%.

The legislation provides for a procedure whereby the company may obtain advance clearance from the Inland Revenue. In practice it will always be necessary for the company to obtain this clearance.

4 Tax planning for directors and employees

Are there still tax advantages in giving employees benefits rather than extra salary?

Employees usually prefer to receive cash which they are free to spend rather than a company benefit which may have less value to them than its real cost. Employers can often obtain advantageous group discount terms for their employees and certain benefits can be provided to employees on advantageous tax terms, including:

- Canteen meals.
- Cars.
- Other assets, such as clothing or furniture.
- Removal expenses, where a move is required for the employment.
- Medical insurance for the lower paid who are not directors (from 6 April 1982).
- Shares under approved option or profit sharing schemes.
- Pensions (considered separately on pages 43 to 44).
- Payments on termination of employment.
- Small loans.
- Living accommodation.

What are the rules for taxing benefits?

Benefits are normally taxable as part of the emoluments of an employment under Schedule E. The general rule is that the benefit taxable upon an employee is the 'money's worth' of the benefit in his or her hands, but this rule is varied for:

- Benefits received by higher-paid employees (earnings at an annual rate of £8,500 or more including expenses and benefits) or by directors.
- Certain specific benefits.

With the above exception employees who are neither higher-paid employees nor directors are taxed under the general rule that a benefit must be money's worth (convertible into money) if it is to rank as a taxable emolument, and it is then taxed on its market value. For example, if a company settles an employee's private expenses of £100, this is treated as £100 income in the hands of the employee. If the company makes available for the use of such an employee an asset such as a television set or a car, and assuming that the employee cannot gain money's worth from possession of the asset, for example by hiring the asset to someone else, or by exchanging it for more salary, the employee will have no taxable benefit.

For higher-paid employees and directors, there is a more stringent general rule for calculating taxable benefits, which is that benefits provided to them or their families by virtue of their employment are taxable on the basis of either the cost to the company or money's worth to the employee, whichever is the greater. The main exceptions to this rule are for company meals provided for staff generally, which are tax free, and company cars, which are taxed at statutory rates well below the real cost of running the car in normal circumstances.

Certain specific benefits are taxable on all employees on a common basis whether or not they are directors or in the higher-paid category. These include goods or services purchased by company vouchers or credit cards, travel tickets, living accommodation, and payments on the termination of employment.

The normal basis of charge for the more common employee benefits is set out in simple terms overleaf, showing separately the charge upon higher-paid employees and directors and upon other employees. The rules are complex, and advice should be taken before implementing any arrangements.

Benefit	*Tax charge for directors and higher-paid employees*	*Tax charge for other employees*
Meals provided directly for all employees by employer on own premises	Tax free	Tax free
Cars made available to employees or members of their families for private use (1)	Scale benefit	Tax free
Assets (other than cars) made available for use of employees or members of their families	20% of market value (4)	Tax free
Reasonable removal expenses caused by employment	Tax free	Tax free
Loans at favourable interest rates	Notional interest (2)	Tax free
Vouchers for cash, goods or services	Cost	Cost
Purchases by company credit cards	Cost of purchases	Cost of purchases from 6 April 1982
Travel tickets (non-business)	Cost	Cost from 6 April 1982
Medical insurance	Cost	Tax free (3)
Living accommodation	Annual value (or rent paid by employer if higher) plus private expenses, if any	Annual value (or rent paid by employer if higher) plus private expenses, if any

Notes

(1) The following section deals with taxation of company cars.
(2) There is a minimum amount of £200 of notional interest which can be assessed.
(3) Tax free after 5 April 1982.
(4) 10% if the asset was first used to provide a benefit before 6 April 1980.

What are the main rules for taxing company cars?

The tax rules relating to company cars are modified in nearly every budget. The main rules for calculating the benefit for the year to 5 April 1983 are as follows:

- Higher-paid employees and directors are assessed according to a table of charges (see the table below), the benefit varying according to the age, cost and engine size of the car.
- As shown in the table, employees who are not directors, and who

are earning at the rate of less than £8,500 (including expenses and benefits) are not assessed to the scale charge.

- Both categories of persons will be assessed (in addition to any scale charge) on private petrol reimbursed, personal liabilities for petrol (or diesel) and oil which are met by the employer (for example, by settlement of personal credit cards) and on any expenditure on private petrol with a company credit card (see below).

Directors and higher-paid employees scale charges for company cars—year to 5 April 1983

	Age of car at end of year of assessment	
	Under 4 years	*4 years or more*
(A) Original market value up to £11,500		
Cylinder capacity:		
1300cc or less	£270	£180
1301—1800cc	£360	£240
more than 1800cc	£540	£360
(B) Original market value over £11,500		
£11,501—£17,300	£780	£528
more than £17,300	£1,260	£840

The 'scale' benefits from the above table are charged at three levels according to the business mileage of the employee during the year:

- At least 18,000 business miles—half scale charge.
- 2,501—17,999 business miles—scale charge.
- 2,500 or fewer miles—scale charge plus half.
- 'Second' cars are assessed at scale charge plus half irrespective of business mileage.
- Petrol provided for private purposes to directors and the higher-paid will be assessed as a benefit in 1983/1984 and future years at scale rates. Meanwhile, it is possible for the employer to provide petrol directly, for example, through the use of a company pump, without any benefit being assessed on the individual. This will not hold true if the individual buys the petrol himself and seeks reimbursement from his employer, or if petrol is purchased using a credit card.

Can the company provide loans to employees?

There are restrictions which, for two categories of individuals, will either prohibit the making of loans or result in tax penalties:

- Company directors—it is illegal in most circumstances for a company to make loans to its directors.

- Company 'participators'—a close company must in nearly all cases pay to the Inland Revenue an amount equal to advance corporation tax (three-sevenths) on making a loan to a participator (generally speaking a shareholder) or to one of his or her 'associates', a term which includes most members of the participator's family.

For other employees, a loan at nil or a low rate of interest can be a valuable benefit. If a loan is used for a qualifying purpose (for example purchase of a main residence) the notional interest benefit (see page 38) will not be charged upon higher-paid employees. The notional interest rate on which tax is paid is generally lower than commercial overdraft rates. Any waiver or release of a loan, irrespective of the rate of interest, would be taxable as employment income.

What are the current rules for taxing payments on termination of employment?

Where an employment is terminated on or after 6 April 1982 payments made on the termination of the employment are taxed on a graduated scale as follows:

- The first £25,000 is tax free.
- The next £25,000 is added to, and treated as the top slice of, the individual's income but the tax payable is reduced by one-half.
- The next £25,000 (£50,001 to £75,000) is then added to income and similarly dealt with but the tax payable is reduced by one-quarter.
- The excess over £75,000 is then added to income and taxed in full at the top rate.

For employments terminated in 1981/1982 the first £25,000 was tax free with the whole of the remainder taxable on the 50% basis.

It is necessary to show that the lump sum payment is made in connection with the termination of the employment. If for instance the payment is a reward or bonus for past services or if the individual has or obtains some entitlement to it from his or her contract of service, it will be fully chargeable to tax as Schedule E income. Payments to shareholders may also be taxable as dividends, and advice should be taken in such cases. Advance arrangements to make lump sum payments on termination of an employment are best avoided, but the Inland Revenue has stated that in normal cases of redundancy it will accept a bona fide termination payment as such, and it invites employers to seek advance clearance in cases of doubt.

The employer is responsible for deducting any tax due on a termination payment under the PAYE system. The employer will normally obtain tax relief for the gross payment as an expense of the trade unless it was not paid for the purposes of the trade, for example, in connection with a takeover or for family reasons.

Is it sensible to allow employees to acquire shares in the company?

This is a commercial question involving striking a balance between retaining the equity of the company within a family and giving employees an incentive interest in the company for which they work.

If a decision is made to allow employees to become shareholders the tax implications are complex and professional advice will always be needed. In general, where the acquisition of options or shares is connected with an employment, the legislation attempts to convert capital growth into income for tax purposes.

There are exceptions which require (amongst other things) that the employee's shares should not have any restrictions attaching to them. To fit within these exceptions it is usually a precondition that the individual buys the shares at market value and funds the acquisition from his or her own resources. There are other exceptions for:

- Shares acquired by employees under an approved option scheme through a SAYE savings contract.
- Shares acquired for employees under 'profit sharing schemes' operated by trustees who use company funds to purchase the company's shares.

From 10 March 1982 an employee who pays interest on a loan

obtained to purchase shares in a close trading company for which he or she works full time will get tax relief for the interest on the loan (see page 32).

Do the same rules for taxing benefits apply both to employees of a company and to employees of an individual or partnership?

Yes. The same rules apply in taxing employee benefits and in relation to employee pension schemes. Employee share schemes necessarily require that the employer is a company.

The annual return of expenses and benefits for directors and higher-paid employees on form P11D is a chore. Can the work be reduced?

Yes. The Inland Revenue can give to an employer dispensations from returning certain expense payments and benefits where the employer can show that there will be no charge to tax in respect of those payments. The most frequent case is the reimbursement of travel expenses, which will normally not give rise to a benefit.

A dispensation will save effort, but will only be given if the Inland Revenue is satisfied that the company's system of controls is adequate to ensure that no tax liability arises. Where company credit cards and vouchers are used to meet expenses, seperate dispensations are required.

My company pays a mileage allowance to employees who use their own cars on business. Do we have to report this to the Inland Revenue?

Yes. It is advisable to agree with the Inland Revenue that the allowance does no more than cover reasonable business expenses. Otherwise, such payments may be emoluments for which the company would have to account for PAYE and National Insurance. This principle also applies to allowances such as subsistence allowances.

5 Pensions for directors and employees

Are controlling directors subject to special rules for company pension schemes?

All directors, including shareholder directors, may qualify for the full pension benefits available to other employees under approved occupational pension schemes. Although there are restrictions upon the pension entitlements of family company directors, these are not likely to have serious effects unless the director's remuneration is increased substantially in the last two years of his or her working life.

What are the tax rules for contributions to pension schemes?

By 'pension schemes' are meant schemes approved by the Inland Revenue under the Finance Act 1970. These are known as 'exempt approved schemes', and they are entitled to a number of tax reliefs:

- Contributions by an employer are deductible in computing his or her taxable profits.
- Employees can get a tax deduction for their contributions up to 15% of their remuneration.
- Income and capital gains of the pension fund are exempt from tax.
- Life assurance cover can be arranged so that proceeds are exempt from capital transfer tax.
- A tax free lump sum can be paid at retirement.

Does this mean that employers' contributions to pension schemes are unrestricted?

Pension schemes approved by the Inland Revenue have a built-in restriction because the benefits must be within certain limits. The contributions payable must not exceed those necessary to provide the scheme benefits. Contributions are virtually unrestricted up to these limits.

What are the benefits allowed?

These include:

- A pension at normal retirement age of up to two-thirds final salary.
- Part of the pension may be exchanged for a lump sum of up to one and a half times final salary.
- On death a pension for the spouse of up to four-ninths of employee's final salary.
- A lump sum on death in service of up to four times salary.
- Pensions may be increased in line with the Retail Price Index.

There are a number of concessions given in special circumstances which can increase these limits.

Why is a pension scheme for employees able to provide more generous benefits than a self-employed individual's retirement annuity scheme?

Because of the cost few private schemes maintained by small businesses are funded to provide the maximum allowable benefits. For employers wishing to provide the maximum benefits, however, there is virtually no restriction on their contributions provided that the scheme can absorb further funding, although the Inland Revenue may insist on spreading the tax relief on an exceptional single premium over several years. This contrasts with the retirement annuity rules for the self-employed where allowable contributions are normally limited to 17½% or 20% of taxable profits for each year (see page 26).

How does a pension scheme fit into personal financial planning?

A pension scheme does not provide a full investment programme for an individual, although in most cases it will be an essential part of any individual's savings arrangements. The provision of a regular pension on retirement is not just a safeguard but enhances the individual's freedom to settle his or her personal capital, including any capital derived from selling his or her business on retirement. The benefits can include both life assurance and substantial lump sums payable tax free on retirement. An approved pension scheme is by far the most tax efficient method of saving.

Shareholder directors of family companies may also be interested in self-administered pension schemes. Under such a scheme, provision may be made for part of the funds to be invested in or lent back to the business. This can overcome, to some extent, the objection that pension fund monies are lost to a company once they are paid over, but at the expense of some risk to the security of the pension.

Pensions planning is a specialist field and expert advice must be obtained on such matters as the benefits of a particular scheme, the relative advantages of using an insurance company or having a self-administered scheme, and negotiation with the Inland Revenue Superannuation Funds Office.

6 Looking to the future

I am seriously considering the future of my company. What are the main tax considerations?

These will depend on the decisions taken concerning not only the commercial future of the business but also the needs of the proprietor and his or her family. The choices will include:

- An outright sale of the company.
- A partial sale either by private placing or by flotation.
- Planning to pass control of the company intact to the next generation of the family.
- Splitting up the company into different constituent businesses in the hands of different members of the family or different shareholders.

Similar options will face the head of a family partnership or a sole trader, although an unincorporated business is unlikely to be as easily marketable as shares in a family company. In all cases it is important to seek professional advice at the earliest opportunity, particularly if it is the intention to preserve the business into the next generation.

If I sell the company, is there any way of avoiding capital gains tax? I am not keen on schemes which are entirely artificial.

If the shares are sold to another company which acquires at least 25% of the ordinary shares, any capital gains tax liability can be deferred by accepting either shares or loan stock in the purchasing company in consideration for the shares being sold. The tax is deferred until the new shares or stock are ultimately sold. Otherwise any profit arising on the sale of the shares will be chargeable to capital gains tax at the rate of 30%, subject to the 'retirement relief' mentioned below. If part of the consideration is satisfied in shares and part in cash, then the capital gains tax liability is restricted to the chargeable gain attributable to the shares disposed of for cash.

Is it sensible to take shares and/or loan stock in lieu of cash in these circumstances?

This is really an investment decision. If the shares being offered by the purchaser are an attractive investment and readily realisable should cash be required in the future, then there is every reason to defer the tax liability. However, if a spread of investments is required, it may be necessary to sell at least a part of the holding for cash.

What often happens is that the vendors of a private company take shares in the purchaser and then realise only sufficient shares each year to ensure that any chargeable gain is within the annual capital gains tax exemption limit (currently £5,000). If gifts of shares or stock are first made to different members of the family other than the donor's spouse, the donor and the recipient can elect to roll over the gain (see page 49). The recipient can then realise the gain free of capital gains tax up to his or her exemption limit. For the gifts to be free of capital transfer tax the donor's exemption levels for capital transfer tax should not be exceeded.

Are there any other reliefs available to reduce the capital gains tax liability on a sale?

Retirement relief may be available for gains up to £50,000 where the shareholder is at least 60 years of age. To get the maximum relief the shares have to be sold after the shareholder is 65, and the relief is restricted, on a sliding scale, according to ages between 60 and 65. There are further conditions in that the retiring shareholder must own 25% of the company's voting shares (or 5% owned by the retiring shareholder and a minimum of more than 45% owned by members of his or her family), and to get full relief he or she must have been in full time working employment with the company for at least 10 years.

Similar relief is available for business assets owned by the sole trader and partner.

Should I enter into artificial schemes to avoid capital gains tax on sale?

Only if all the risks of litigation are accepted. Recent decisions in the House of Lords have meant that the chances of success for most schemes are small.

What is the situation on a partial sale or flotation?

The same rules outlined above will apply. The chargeable gain on the shares sold or released to the market will be liable to capital gains tax in the normal way.

I have heard about the Unlisted Securities Market. Could I realise a part of my shareholding in this way?

The Unlisted Securities Market is a facility offered by the Stock Exchange to enable shareholders of private and other relatively small companies to sell shares to the public and obtain an unofficial quotation for their shares without being subjected to rules as rigorous as those governing companies with fully listed securities. It is often a half-way house before full quotation and is becoming increasingly popular for family companies.

As little as 10% of the company's equity capital can be made available to the market in this way (depending on the way in which the shares are to be offered to the public). Capital gains tax will be payable on chargeable gains arising on the shares sold.

Can I raise cash by arranging for my company to buy in some of my shares?

This is unlikely to be feasible except in very limited circumstances. However it may be worth looking at if the company is a trading company and Inland Revenue clearance can be obtained. The company will need to be able to show that the transaction is designed to benefit its trade, as well as meeting a number of other conditions of approval, the most important of which is that after the transaction the seller of the shares (and his or her 'associates' including close relatives) may not retain more than 30% of the company. Although as yet there is no experience to go on, it is likely to be more difficult for a company to put up a convincing commercial case to buy in the shares of a controlling shareholder than it will be to buy in the shares, for instance, of a minority shareholder who may be considered a nuisance. Any reasonable case, however, may be worth trying.

If Revenue approval is obtained, the shareholder's profit (if any) on sale of the shares is brought into his or her capital gains tax computation. If clearance is not obtained the proceeds paid by the company will be treated as a dividend and taxed accordingly, to the extent that they are not merely repayments of the original amounts subscribed for the shares.

If I transfer shares or business interests to members of my family in the next generation, will I have to pay both capital gains tax and capital transfer tax?

A short answer to this question is 'not necessarily', because a donor and donee can elect jointly that no charge to capital gains tax will arise on the transfer. The transfer will be chargeable to capital transfer tax but there are a number of reliefs which may remove or reduce the liability. These rules are worth explaining in more detail.

A gift of shares (or other assets) is treated as a disposal at market value for capital gains tax purposes, and a liability can arise if the value of the shares exceeds their cost (as adjusted by the 'indexation allowance' given by the Finance Act 1982).

If a gift is made by one individual resident in the United Kingdom to another, a claim may be made for the gain to be 'held over'. This claim, which must be made by both the donor and the recipient, means that the donor does not become liable to tax on his or her notional gain, whilst the recipient is treated as acquiring the asset at its market value less the amount of the donor's notional gain which has been held over. Tax will arise when the new owner sells the shares, and there are rules which trigger off the gain if the new owner becomes non-resident.

The relief is often referred to as 'rollover relief'. It is also available when gifts are made to trustees provided that the donor and the trustees are resident in the United Kingdom. Trustees and beneficiaries may also make a claim, for example, in circumstances where trust assets are transferred to a beneficiary.

If the shares or business assets pass on death there is no capital gains tax charge, and the beneficiaries acquire the shares at their market value at the date of death and not at the original cost to the deceased. This is more beneficial for capital gains tax than adopting the 'rollover' treatment mentioned above but capital transfer tax payable on death will be at rates which are considerably higher than those which apply to lifetime gifts (see table on page 51).

Now that rollover relief can be used to defer payment of capital gains tax the tax costs of rearranging interests in a family business during the lifetime of the proprietor are often found to be fairly manageable. We give an example of this on page 55.

On a commercial sale of shares, capital transfer tax will not normally arise because the seller is only exchanging one asset for another and there is unlikely to be any element of gift in the transaction. There may well be a charge to capital gains tax.

What is meant by indexation of capital gains tax?

The Finance Act 1982 has introduced a new rule whereby a person (whether individual or company) disposing of an asset after 6 April 1982 may add to his or her cost in the capital gains tax computation an amount known as an indexation allowance.

The indexation allowance is only given on assets which have been held for more than 12 months. It is calculated by reference to movements in the Retail Price Index from the later of March 1982 or 12 months after the date of acquisition of the assets. This rule means that relief is given neither for past inflation (before March 1982) nor for inflation during the first year of ownership. The value of the allowance for disposals in the immediate future is therefore limited.

There are complex rules for identification of shares where the taxpayer has bought shares of the same class at different times. Generally speaking, the taxpayer's shares are identified on a first in last out basis which, needless to say, is the least favourable. There are also rules which prevent the taxpayer obtaining relief for a 'loss' where his or her proceeds of sale are more than the original cost but less than the original cost plus the indexation allowance.

What are the rates of capital transfer tax?

Capital transfer tax is charged on a sliding scale of rates on what are called 'chargeable transfers'. Broadly speaking, chargeable transfers are those which reduce the transferor's estate and are not specifically exempt. They will include lifetime gifts and the transfer of an individual's estate on death. The rate of tax payable is fixed by reference to the individual transferor's cumulative total of chargeable transfers within the preceding 10 years.

For transfers made on or after 9 March 1982 the lifetime rates are significantly lower than those applying on death. For the transfer to qualify for the lower rates the donor must survive the transfer by at least three years. The following is the current table of rates.

Cumulative chargeable transfers (after exemptions and reliefs) Lower limit £	Upper limit £	*Transfers on death or within three years of death* Rate %	*Lifetime transfers* Rate %
0	55,000	Nil	Nil
55,000	75,000	30	15
75,000	100,000	35	17½
100,000	130,000	40	20
130,000	165,000	45	22½
165,000	200,000	50	25
200,000	250,000	55	30
250,000	650,000	60	35
650,000	1,250,000	65	40
1,250,000	2,500,000	70	45
2,500,000+		75	50

What are the main reliefs from capital transfer tax?

The most important of the capital transfer tax rules which can limit the tax charge on a chargeable transfer are:

- Chargeable transfers, whether made in lifetime or on death, up to a cumulative total of £55,000 for each individual, are chargeable at a nil rate and are thus free of tax.
- After 10 years have elapsed following a chargeable transfer, its value ceases to form part of the cumulative total of transfers by reference to which the rates of capital transfer tax are fixed for the future.
- Transfers of up to £3,000 per annum are wholly exempt. This exemption is available to both spouses so that for husband and wife the total figure is £6,000 per annum. The value of this exemption is effectively doubled if business property relief (see below) is

also available.

- Transfers, regardless of the number made in any one year, are exempt if no single donee receives more than £250.
- Transfers between husband and wife are wholly exempt unless the transfer is made by a spouse who is domiciled in the United Kingdom to a spouse who is not. In this case, there is a £55,000 limit to the exemption.
- £5,000 can be given away free of tax by both husband and wife to each of their children on, or in consideration of, their marriage. The equivalent exemption for gifts by grandparents is £2,500.
- Regular transfers out of surplus income which do not affect the transferor's standard of living can be made free of tax.

What are the main reliefs relating to businesses?

Provided certain conditions as to period of ownership are met, 50% of the value of a business or of the shares transferred by a shareholder with a majority holding in a trading company at the time of the transfer will be relieved from charge to capital transfer tax. This is known as 'business property relief'.

The rate relating to transfers made by minority shareholders in unquoted companies is 20%. There is also a 30% relief applying to transfers of certain assets used by a company which the transferor controls, by a business carried on by the transferor, or by a partnership in which the transferor is a partner.

Shares in an investment company will not qualify for business property relief unless it is acting merely as a holding company for trading subsidiaries.

How does control of a company affect my liability to capital transfer tax?

A gift out of a controlling shareholding in a company will be eligible to the higher 50% rate of business property relief, as explained above. However, value attaches to control of a company, and a majority shareholding (that is, one comprising more than 50% of the voting shares) will often have a substantially higher market value per share than a minority holding, to which the 20% rate of relief applies.

Can you explain this more fully?

The valuation of unquoted or unlisted shares (and in certain cases quoted shares as well) is related to the influence that the holding gives the owner over the affairs of the company. A shareholder who controls more than half the voting shares has control over the earnings and distributions of the company. The valuation of his or her holding will be made by reference to, or by taking account of, the full earnings of the company.

If the holding does not give the owner control, or any degree of influence, it is likely to be valued on the basis of the dividends which can reasonably be expected or (in some cases) hoped for in the future. Most companies pay dividends which are a fraction of earnings and many private companies pay no dividends at all. Valuations of a minority holding in a private company on a dividend yield basis will come to a different, and generally much lower, value per share than valuations on a full earnings basis.

Does this mean that a gift of shares which allows control to pass will be expensive in terms of capital transfer tax?

Very often it will be. Capital transfer tax is payable on the amount by which the transferor's estate is reduced by making the gift, and a gift which involves the donor losing control of a company can reduce the value of the donor's estate far more than the value of benefit given to the recipient.

How is this calculated?

If, for example, an individual holds 51% of a company and gives away a 2% holding, the amount of the reduction in that individual's estate will be equal to the difference between:

- A 51% shareholding valued on say a full earnings basis, and
- A 49% shareholding valued by reference to expected dividend yield.

This difference is likely to be a much larger figure than the value to the recipient of a 2% holding, unless the recipient personally obtains control.

Can tax on this value attributed to control be alleviated?

To some extent, yes. Since the amount attributable to loss of control will usually be the same irrespective of the number of shares transferred it normally pays to transfer a large block of shares to maximise the benefit from the higher (50%) rate of business property relief.

Could I not lose control by transferring shares to my spouse?

It will do no good for this purpose. Under what is known as the 'related property' rule, shares owned by husband and wife have to be valued on the basis that they form a single holding. If they jointly control the company a gift of shares by either of them (except a gift to each other) will be valued on the basis of a controlling interest. However, they could both be entitled to the higher 50% rate of business property relief if they have held their respective shareholdings for at least two years.

Do the same principles apply for quoted as for unquoted shares?

The valuation of quoted shares will depend on the quoted price although there will often be a premium ascribed to a controlling interest.

Business property relief at the rate of 50% may be attributed to a controlling interest in a quoted company but no relief is given for a minority interest.

Shares listed on the Unlisted Securities Market are not treated as 'quoted' for tax purposes. The listed price will be the basis of valuation (with some premium for control), but for such shares business property relief may be available both for a controlling interest (at 50%) and a minority interest (20%).

If I wish to keep the business in the family, what should I be doing now?

Now that most gifts can be made free of capital gains tax, the main concern will be to limit any liability to capital transfer tax. You should calculate the size of the potential liability, and then look at possible methods of reducing it, for example by:

• Taking advantage of the lower lifetime rates of tax by spreading the interests in the business as widely as possible within the family, particularly amongst members of the next or later generations. Where the members of the latest generation are still in infancy a transfer to trustees for their benefit may be appropriate (see page 58).
• Ensuring that transfers qualify for all possible reliefs and that the values on which tax will be levied are as low as possible.
• Making maximum use of all available exemptions.

You should then consider how any remaining tax liability is to be paid without jeopardising the future of the business, for example, by the use of life assurance policies (see page 57).

What is the best way of achieving the objectives mentioned above?

Since worthwhile savings in capital transfer tax can be achieved by making lifetime gifts of assets which are expected to increase in value, it will pay to transfer shares to the next generation as early as possible in the company's development. If a new trading activity is planned, the creation of a new company to undertake it, in which the next generation can take an interest from the start may, if the activity is successful, have substantial tax saving benefits.

Full use should be made of the £3,000 annual exemption available to all shareholders. For as long as a husband and wife have control, then the 50% rate of business property relief will be available to each spouse (provided that he or she has held the shares for at least two years) so that the value that may be transferred tax free each year by husband and wife together is £12,000.

	Husband £	*Wife* £	*Total* £
Value of shares transferred	6,000	6,000	12,000
Business property relief (50%)	3,000	3,000	6,000
	3,000	3,000	6,000
Annual exemption	3,000	3,000	6,000
Chargeable to tax	£Nil	£Nil	£Nil

By planning for a programme of regular gifts over a period of time, and using the annual and other exemptions, a substantial proportion of the value of the business can be transferred to the next generation entirely free of tax.

As both husband and wife can claim capital transfer tax reliefs and exemptions, and the benefit of the nil and lower rate bands of tax, lifetime gifts between them may be appropriate. By this means they can each make full use of the reliefs.

Can you give an example of what might be achieved by taking advantage of the spouse and annual exemptions and the nil rate band of tax?

Suppose a taxpayer who is a married man with children owns 100% of the shares in a trading company worth £500,000 which he wishes to pass to his children. Ignoring the value of any other assets he possesses (which would be added to the above figure when fixing the rate of capital transfer tax payable), tax of £87,500 at current rates would be payable on his death or, if all his property were left to his wife, on her subsequent death.

Were the taxpayer to transfer a part of his shareholding to his wife, they would both be in a position to make use of the £3,000 annual exemption and the nil rate band of tax. After the wife had owned the shares given to her for two years, she would be eligible to the business property relief as well as her husband. In no more than three years, a substantial interest in the business could be transferred to the next generation free of tax. Ignoring any changes in the value of the shares in this period and assuming that the taxpayer and his wife wish to retain control of the company the following situation might be achieved.

	Husband £	*Wife* £	*Total* £
Shares divided between husband and wife	300,000	200,000	500,000
Gifts to children £55,000 nil rate band gross of 50% business property relief (a)	110,000	110,000	220,000
	190,000	90,000	280,000
Annual exempt gifts of £3,000 to children gross of 50% business property relief, for three years	18,000	9,000(b)	27,000
Value of residual shareholdings after 3 years	£172,000	£81,000	£253,000

Notes

(a) Wife's gift to be made only after she has held the shares for two complete years.
(b) Wife's annual gifts restricted to prevent loss of joint control.

Were the survivor of the husband and wife in the above example to live for 10 years following the £110,000 gifts to the children, and assuming that he or she had inherited the deceased spouse's residual interest, capital transfer tax liability on the second death would amount to £25,350. This shows a total saving of £62,150 (£87,500 less £25,350). On the other hand, were they each to leave their residual holdings direct to their children rather than to each other, then the tax liability on death could be reduced even further.

This example illustrates the savings that could be achieved by planning over a long period, although it is accepted that there are circumstances where this is not possible.

What part can life assurance play in planning for capital transfer tax on my business?

Life assurance is well suited to provide for capital transfer tax liabilities:

- It is a tax efficient savings medium not only because, within limits, the taxpayer pays only 85% of the premium due, the Inland Revenue providing the balance, but also because insurance company funds enjoy beneficial rates of tax.
- Once the policy is in force, the basic sum assured is guaranteed.
- If the tax liability will not arise until the death of the survivor of the husband and wife (because the survivor inherits all under the will of the first to die), a joint life and survivor policy will ensure that the funds are available when needed. The level of premiums on such policies takes account of the age of the younger spouse.
- If the policy is written in trust for the benefit of the younger generation (or, alternatively, if a member of the younger generation effects the policy on the life of a parent) the policy proceeds themselves can be received free of capital transfer tax on the life assured's death.

Other points relating to the use of life policies are:

- Depending on the age of the life to be assured, a with-profits policy will usually be appropriate because the bonus additions will assist in providing for any increasing tax liability as the business itself expands.

- Where a policy is written in trust for the younger generation, the annual premiums will be regarded as annual gifts in their favour by the person paying them. These will not, however, generate a charge to capital transfer tax if they fall within the annual £3,000 exemption or, alternatively, the surplus income exemption.

- The premiums on policies effected by the younger generation on a parent's life may be financed by, for example, increasing the level of salary they draw from the business or distributing profits to them by way of dividend.

- Trustees can, if the trust deed permits, use income to meet premiums due on policies on the settlor's life.

Might trusts have a part to play in capital transfer tax planning for my business?

Although trusts no longer have quite the tax planning advantages once associated with them there are many occasions when they can be very useful. For example, trusts for the benefit of minor members of the family which are drawn up in certain terms receive beneficial tax treatment and can be used to hold shares in the family company. The following benefits may be obtained:

- Any future increase in value in the shares given to the trustees for the benefit of the younger generation on their attaining full age will be free of capital transfer tax.

- Dividends on the shares being accumulated by the trustees for the ultimate benefit of the younger generation will suffer income tax at the maximum rate of 45%. The funds represented by income accumulations might themselves be used to good effect, for example, by the trustees acquiring further shares from the older generation or, alternatively, by the trustees taking out life assurance on the settlor's life.

Trustees of discretionary settlements are liable to both capital transfer tax and capital gains tax so they are no longer natural vehicles for tax avoidance. However trustees can now claim capital gains tax hold over relief (see page 49) and there have been recent changes for the better in the capital transfer tax rules applying to this type of trust, so that discretionary settlements (particularly those of limited value) may continue to have some uses.

Limited discretionary trusts created under wills can offer considerable flexibility to the deceased shareholder's executors and family to deal with the deceased's business interests in the most tax efficient way following his or her death. All trusts and particularly discretionary will trusts must be carefully drafted if capital transfer tax and other problems are to be avoided in the future. Professional advice is always necessary.

If my children are already shareholders, can I allocate a part of the business to them and retain another part myself without tax penalty?

Breaking up an existing business into two or more separate businesses is not a simple operation and will always involve incurring substantial professional costs. It may be possible to create two or more companies to acquire separate trades, their shares then being exchanged for shares in the existing company. A reorganisation on these lines might be possible without creating an unacceptable tax liability either by liquidating the existing company or under the 'demerger' provisions of the tax legislation.

How important is it to my business to have a will?

If an individual does not leave a will, his property, including his business interests, will pass to the heirs in accordance with the rules relating to intestate estates. These rules may result in a wholly unsatisfactory situation developing after the person's death. Although it is now possible to vary the effects of these rules after the death if all the beneficiaries are of full age and agree, this can be a complex matter and all individuals, but particularly those with interests in family businesses, should have a will and review it periodically.

A will need not be regarded as being an inflexible instruction to executors to deal with the estate in a given way. The will could include wide discretionary powers. In addition, it is now possible for the executors and the adult beneficiaries to agree to vary the terms of a will, without capital transfer tax penalty, if its terms prove to be unsatisfactory for any reason. This facility which must be exercised within two years of the date of death can be a useful one if the will creates problems for the survivors in ensuring the continuity of the family business.

What is the most important factor in tax planning for the future of my business?

Simply, start as soon as possible. Problems usually arise only in circumstances where planning is left until the last moment.

If the members of the elder generation start to transfer their interests in the family business whilst they are comparatively young and before the full potential of the business is realised, the ultimate saving in capital transfer tax will be that much greater. A programme of lifetime transfers might be supplemented by the use of life assurance. If proper provision is made for retirement pensions it may be much easier to release capital to the next generation.

Lastly, this is a complex topic. The comments set out in this chapter of the book have touched only briefly on the problems and solutions to them. Professional advice must be taken.

Index